NEW YORK

TRAVEL JOURNAL

UNPLUG & WRITE

WANDERLUST

A VERY STRONG

DESIRE TO

TRAVEL

WANDERLUST JOURNALS COLLECTION

WWW.WANDERLUST-JOURNALS.COM

INDEX

IF FOUND

PLEASE RETURN IT TO:

Name:

Address:

Phone number:

Email address:

Trip Planner

W?

What? (Do I want to learn from this trip)

When? (Do I travel?)

Where? (Do I go?)

Why? (Do I travel?)

CHECKLIST

THINGS TO DO BEFORE LEAVING

Family and Friends

Telephone numbers

(in case I lose my phone)

Packing list

Things I'm taking with me

Carry-on
Important Documents and Necessities

Hygiene and medicine

Clothing

Miscellaneous

Itinerary Overview

MAPS

(PASTE MAP)

My favourite landscapes

My favourite museums

Restaurants I love

MY CHILLOUT PLACES

SERENDIPITOUS TRAVEL MOMENTS:

Serendipity is an unexpected discovery when we are seeking something different.
The word emerged in 1700 from a Persian fairy tale, which takes place on an island called "Serendip", in which the protagonists solved all their problems through coincidences.

WHAT IS MY SERENDIPITOUS MOMENT IN THIS TRIP?

Things I do while traveling but not at home:

SONGS THAT INSPIRE ME ON THIS TRIP:

CULTURAL SHOCK
(THINGS, PEOPLE, HABITS I'M NOT USED TO SEE)

Mood Tracker

Things that make me happy:

Things that make me sad:

Things that make me angry:

Things that make me Calm:

Color me when
stressed
(or waiting at the airport)

DRAW WHATEVER IS MISSING

DRAW WHATEVER IS MISSING

My takeaway of this trip is:

I HAVE LEARNED...

FOR NEXT TRIP I WOULD AVOID...

WHAT I LIKED THE MOST...

Countries I have visited in my life...

(TO FILL IN)

MY BEST PHOTOS

WHEN?

WHERE?

WHEN?

WHERE?

WHEN?

WHERE?

WHEN?

WHERE?

Wonderful people I met on this trip

NAME:

EMAIL:

COUNTRY:

HE / SHE MADE MY TRIP SPECIAL

BECAUSE...

NAME:

EMAIL:

COUNTRY:

HE / SHE MADE MY TRIP SPECIAL

BECAUSE...

Name:

Email:

Country:

He / She Made my trip special

because...

Name:

Email:

Country:

He / She Made my trip special

because...

My thoughts

MY CREATIVE SPACE

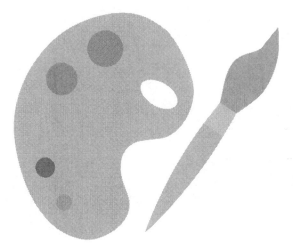

Thanks for leaving a review for this book

or sending us your feedback to:

contact@wanderlust-journals.com

Don't forget to Check out

The Wanderlust Journals collection

We have a journal for every moment of your life

Get 30%off

On your next Wanderlust Journal

CODE: 4CTLX2K3

INSTRUCTIONS:

- Scan the QR CODE (or just enter Createspace store and search Wanderlust journals)
- In the checkout insert the code: 4CTLX2K3 and automatically save 30% in your purchase.

Made in the USA
San Bernardino, CA
08 March 2020